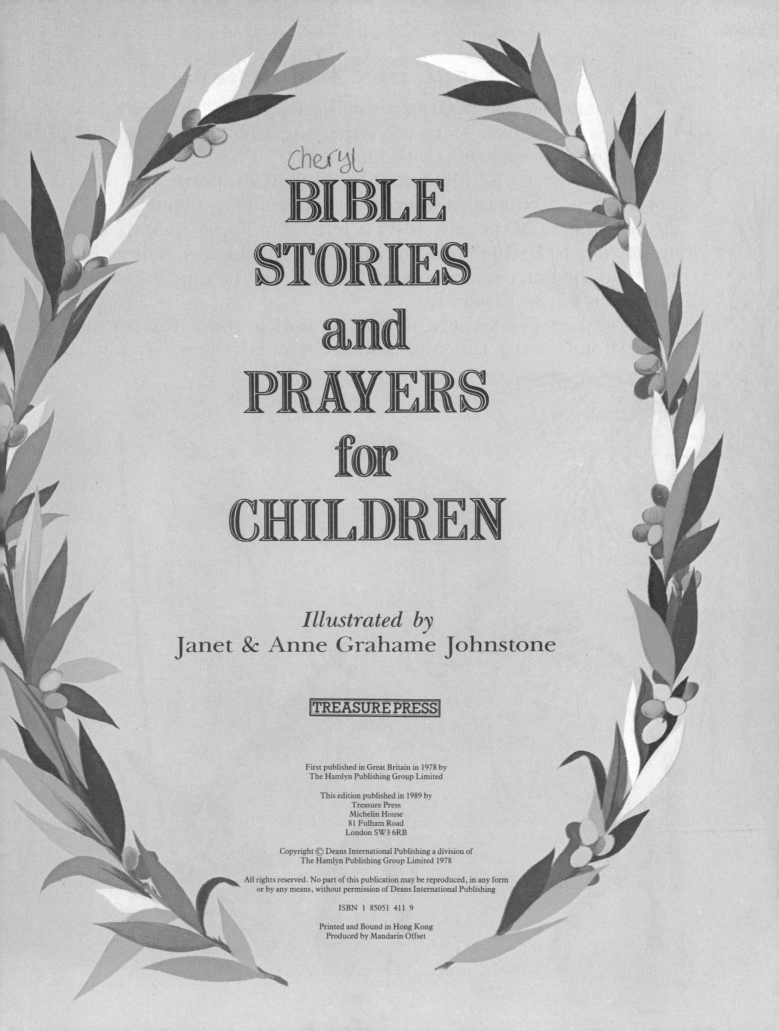

cheryl

BIBLE STORIES and PRAYERS for CHILDREN

Illustrated by
Janet & Anne Grahame Johnstone

TREASURE PRESS

First published in Great Britain in 1978 by
The Hamlyn Publishing Group Limited

This edition published in 1989 by
Treasure Press
Michelin House
81 Fulham Road
London SW3 6RB

Copyright © Deans International Publishing a division of
The Hamlyn Publishing Group Limited 1978

ISBN 1 85051 411 9

Printed and Bound in Hong Kong
Produced by Mandarin Offset

Arrival in Bethlehem

MARY and Joseph lived in a small town called Nazareth. Joseph was a carpenter. Mary was expecting a baby. One day Joseph came in from his workshop with some news.

"We must go to Bethlehem. The Roman Emperor has ordered everyone to go to the town where he was born, to be taxed."

A week later, Mary and Joseph left their home to start on the long journey to Bethlehem. They travelled by donkey. The road was rough and the journey very uncomfortable. By the time they reached Bethlehem they were very tired.

They looked everywhere, trying to find a room for the night. All the hotels were full and nobody wanted them. At last they

persuaded an inn-
keeper to let
them sleep in
his stable.

The Birth of Jesus

THE stable was warm with the breath of the cattle. The floor was covered with hay and the donkeys and oxen stood quietly in their stalls. The innkeeper had given Joseph a candle which was standing on a stool in one corner. It sent soft shadows around the bare walls.

Mary knew that very soon the baby God had sent her would be born. What could she use for a cot? She looked around the stable. There, at the far end, was the manger from which normally the cattle ate. Mary decided to use it. She started to make a comfortable bed of the soft sweet hay.

Later that night, when all was very quiet except for the gentle sound of the wind among the trees, Mary's baby was born. He was a little boy and Mary called him Jesus, as God had told her. She had no clothes for him, so she wrapped him in a plain strip of material and laid him in the bed she had made in the manger.

The Shepherds

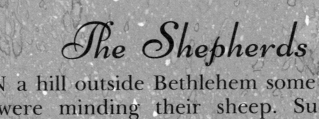

ON a hill outside Bethlehem some shepherds were minding their sheep. Suddenly an angel appeared telling them to go to the stable and find the baby Jesus. When they found him they knelt and worshipped him.

Adoration of the Magi

ON the evening when Jesus was born three clever and important men were talking together. One of them was standing gazing at the lovely starry sky. Suddenly he pointed to a star which was much brighter than the rest.

"That is the star we have been waiting for," he said.

The other two men were very excited.

"It's the star which tells us the baby Jesus has been born. We'll go and worship him."

They set off for the king's palace. They were sure that was where they would find Jesus. But when they got there the king said he knew nothing about the baby.

"If you find him come back and tell me," he said.

The three men went on their journey. The star led them all the way to the stable. Then it stopped.

"He can't be in there," said the men.

But they went in very quietly. Over in the corner a little light was shining. And there was the baby Jesus, with Mary and Joseph.

The three wise men knelt down and gave him the beautiful presents they had brought. Then they said a 'thank you' prayer to God because they knew that God had sent his son to tell people that he loved them.

The Flight into Egypt

AFTER the three wise men had left the stable it was very quiet. Mary looked at Jesus lovingly.

"How lucky we are, Joseph," she whispered, "to be allowed to look after God's own baby."

Joseph nodded.

"Yes, Mary, we are. But come now, it's time for bed. Tomorrow we must start on the long journey back to Nazareth."

But that night God spoke to Joseph in a dream. He told him not to return to Nazareth, but to go to Egypt, because the King wanted to kill Jesus.

The next day Joseph told Mary of his dream.

"We must go as quickly as possible," he said. "We must keep Jesus safe."

Mary, Joseph and the baby left Bethlehem that evening.

Mary rode on the donkey with Jesus and Joseph walked in front. It was a dark and frightening journey. They had to travel at night so that no one would tell King Herod they were escaping. It took them a long time, but at last they got there and found a house where they could live. Joseph built a workshop for his carpentry and they lived there for several happy years. Then, one night, Joseph had another dream. God said:

"Joseph, King Herod has died so you can go back to Nazareth now and take Mary and Jesus with you."

Jesus in the Temple

ONE day, when Jesus was twelve years old, he rushed into his father's workshop.

"Father! We're nearly ready to leave!"

His parents were taking him to the Festival at Jerusalem. They were travelling with a group of friends and relations.

Never had Jesus seen so many people as there were when they arrived in Jerusalem. He had so many questions to ask, and so much to talk about that the time went much too quickly. His parents smiled at his excitement. But when it was time to go home they could not find him.

"He must be with the other children," they said, as the donkeys moved forward.

But that night they discovered he was not in the group at all.

"We must go back and look for him," said Mary.

So Mary and Joseph went back to Jerusalem. They looked everywhere but could not find him.

"Let's go to the Temple and ask if anyone has seen him," said Mary.

When they went into the temple they were very surprised. Jesus was sitting quite happily talking to the priests.

"Why didn't you stay with us?" asked Mary. "We have looked for you every-where."

"Didn't you know you would find me in God's house? I have work to do for him," Jesus answered. "But I'm ready now."

And he went back to Nazareth with Joseph and Mary.

The Palsied Man

WHEN Jesus was grown up he was teaching in a small house one day. There was a crowd of people in the room trying to listen. There were a lot more outside.

While Jesus was talking four men arrived with a sick man lying on a stretcher. They tried to push their way through the crowd so that they could reach Jesus, but the more they tried the more the crowd blocked the doorway.

"It's impossible," said one of the men. "We won't be able to see Jesus today."

"I've a good idea," said another.

He led them round to the back of the house to some stairs. They climbed up on to the roof, lifting the stretcher very gently.

"What do we do now?" asked another man.
"If we move some tiles we can make a hole. Then we will be right above Jesus."

"I don't think we ought," argued the first man. "Why don't we come back another day when Jesus is less busy?"

"But Jesus always has a crowd of people with him. I'm sure he will heal our friend when he sees the trouble we have taken."

And so, very quietly and carefully, the four friends began to move the tiles away. Soon they had made a big hole in the roof and they could see Jesus sitting in the room below. He was talking to the large crowd, and because they were listening to him, nobody had noticed what was going on above them. Jesus was telling them how much God loved them.

"It is because God loves you that he sent me, his son, to teach you and to heal the sick," Jesus said.

When the men on the roof heard this they were very pleased and one of them said:

"Now I'm sure that he will heal our friend. If we tie a piece of rope to each corner of the stretcher we can lower it down right in front of Jesus."

The people in the room below were surprised, but Jesus was pleased the four men had taken so much trouble to bring their friend to see him. He said to the sick man:

"Get up and walk and go home. Your sins are forgiven."

The priests and leaders were very cross.

"Only God can forgive sins," they said.

But when the man stood up and started to walk they were amazed and said to each other:

"This man Jesus really must be God's messenger if he can heal people and forgive sins."

Then the healed man walked home, and wherever he went he told people how wonderful Jesus was.

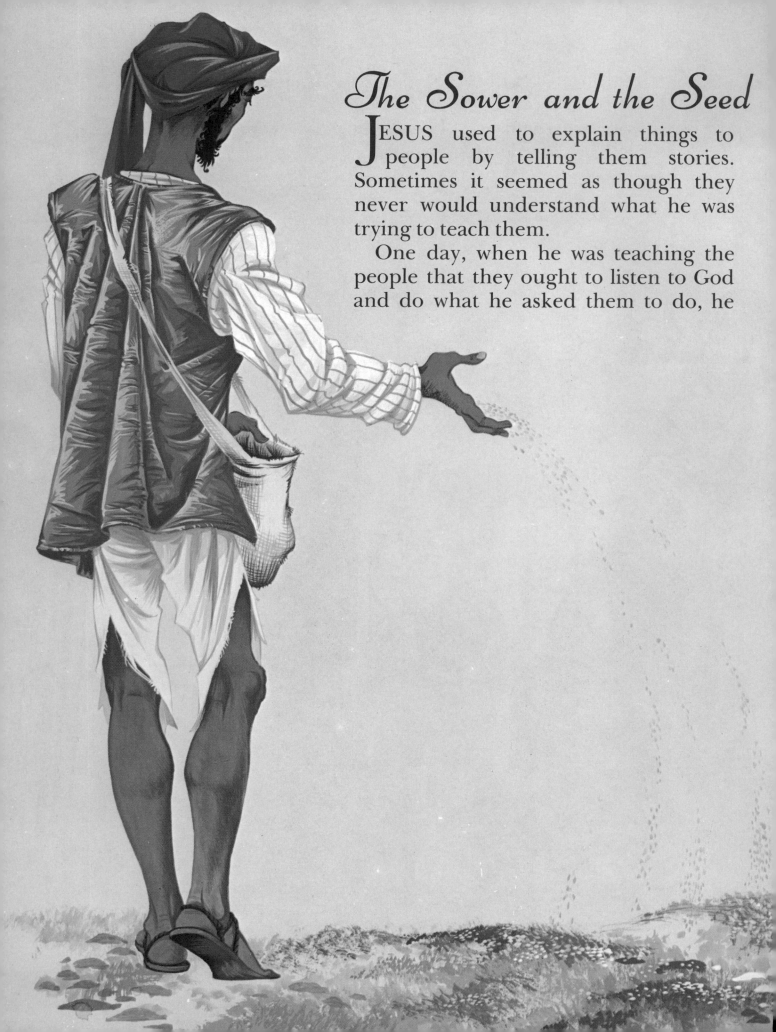

The Sower and the Seed

JESUS used to explain things to people by telling them stories. Sometimes it seemed as though they never would understand what he was trying to teach them.

One day, when he was teaching the people that they ought to listen to God and do what he asked them to do, he told them this story:

A sower went out into a field to sow some seed. As he walked along he scattered the seed first to the right and then to the left and it fell on to the ground around him. Some of it fell on the path where there was no earth, and it could not grow. But it did not stay there for long because the birds flew down and ate it.

"This," explained Jesus, "is like the people who don't listen to God when he speaks to them."

Then some of the seed fell on to the stony ground, where it began to grow. But it had no roots and when the sun came out the little shoots were so weak that they withered away and died.

"This," Jesus said, "is like the people who listen to what God tells them but soon forget all that he says."

Some seed fell into the brambles. When it began to grow the thorns of the brambles got in the way and choked the plants so that they, too, began to die. This is like the people who listen to God and intend to do as he tells them, but soon money and earthly possessions become more important to them.

"But," said Jesus, "a lot of the seed fell on to good earth and it grew until it was very tall. It waved in the breeze like a golden sea. As the sower looked at it he knew that although he had sown it, it had been God's rain and sun on the good earth that had made it so beautiful. These seeds are like the people who listen to God and do as he tells them."

The Centurion and His Servant

ONCE there was a Centurion who lived at Capernaum. He was a very important man who had built the town synagogue, and he was in charge of a lot of men.

One day, one of his servants, whom he liked very much, became

ill. He was so ill that the Centurion was afraid he would die, and he was very worried. He told a friend of his fears.

"What can I do? The doctors say they cannot help him."

"I have heard," his friend told him, "that Jesus is staying in the town. He can make people well. I've seen him do it. Why don't you ask him to heal your servant?"

"I didn't know that Jesus was staying near here. I am sure he will help; he is such a good man. I will send messengers to him straight away."

So the Centurion sent two of his servants to find Jesus.

As they hurried across the town they argued with each other.

"Do you really think that Jesus will be able to cure our friend?" said one. "He is not a doctor and yet I have heard strange stories about him."

"People say," answered the other man, "that he is a very clever and kind man. He is always healing people and teaching them about God. I am sure he can heal our friend."

"But even if he can," argued the first man, "won't he be too busy to come all the way to our master's house? I know our master is a very great man in this town but we cannot really expect Jesus to leave everyone else and come with us."

"I think he will come. From what I have heard Jesus will always help someone who trusts in God."

They had nearly reached the centre of the town now, and they could see the crowds of people who always surrounded Jesus.

"I do hope you are right," the second man said. "It is going to take us a long time to get close enough to talk to him."

Gradually they pushed their way through the crowd until they stood in front of Jesus.

"Master," they said. "Please come with us to the Centurion's house. One of his servants is very ill and he wishes you to save his life."

The messengers were surprised and pleased when Jesus said he would go at once.

As he made his way to the Centurion's house the crowd followed him. When they were not far from the house they saw two more men coming towards them.

"Do you know these men?" asked Jesus.

"Yes," answered the messengers. "They are friends of the Centurion. I wonder what they have to say. Perhaps the servant is already dead."

As the other men reached Jesus one of them began to speak.

"Jesus, our friend, the Centurion, has sent us to tell you not to come any further. He says you are too great a man to come to his house. He knows that you only have to say the words and his servant will be healed. You have no need to come any further."

Jesus was very pleased indeed that the Centurion trusted him so much. He turned to the crowd which was still following him and said:

"I tell you this. I have never found a man before who has so much faith in me."

And so Jesus prayed to God to heal the Centurion's servant, and the messengers went on alone to their master's house.

"Didn't I tell you," one of them said, "that Jesus would be glad to heal our friend?"

They hurried the rest of the way back home and when they reached the house the Centurion came running out to meet them.

"I have such good news," he cried. "My servant is completely well again! Now we must pray and thank God for saving his life!"

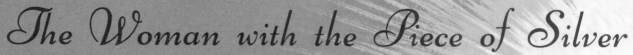

The Woman with the Piece of Silver

ONCE Jesus told a story to explain to everyone how much God loves them.

God is always ready to forgive his people, and he will go on loving and forgiving them even when they don't love him.

Once there was a woman who owned ten silver pieces of money. Each one was worth a great deal and she tried to keep them very safe. One day one of the pieces was missing. She was very worried and began to look for it. She looked in the room where the money was kept. She searched under all the furniture. No, it was not under any of the things in that room.

"Perhaps it has rolled into one of the dark corners where I

cannot see it shine," the woman said.

So she looked in all the corners in the hope of finding the precious piece of silver. But it was not anywhere in that room. She searched in the next room and the next, but still she could not find the money.

"What shall I do?" she said. "Perhaps some of my friends and neighbours will help me find it."

She went to tell her friends about it.

"Of course we'll come and help you," they said. "But why bother so much about one? You still have nine pieces."

"I won't be really happy until I have them all," she replied.

They went to the woman's home. Some searched the house, while others went outside and looked for the money in the courtyard and on the road. It was nearly dark when they returned and still the money had not been found. The woman was very unhappy but she thanked her friends for helping.

"It may be I shall find it, even now," she said. Her friends started on their way home and she went back into the house.

She lit a candle. It sent wavering shadows around the room.

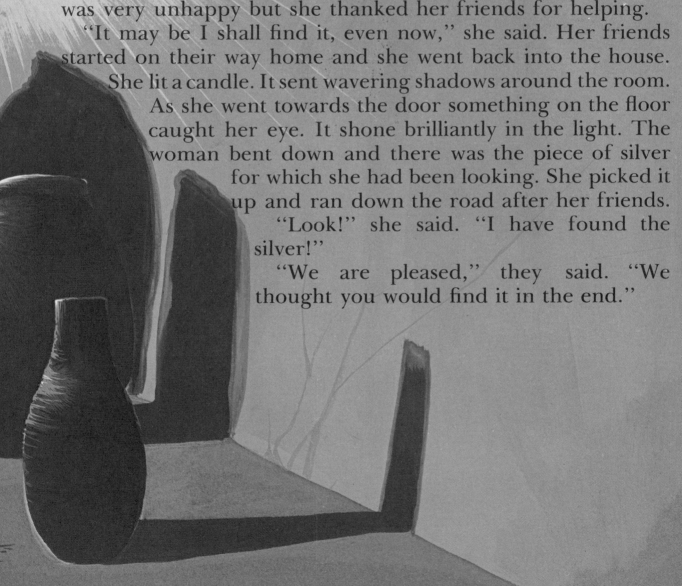

As she went towards the door something on the floor caught her eye. It shone brilliantly in the light. The woman bent down and there was the piece of silver for which she had been looking. She picked it up and ran down the road after her friends.

"Look!" she said. "I have found the silver!"

"We are pleased," they said. "We thought you would find it in the end."

The Prodigal Son

JESUS told a story about a farmer who had two sons. The elder was a great help to his father, and worked hard. But the younger son was an impatient boy. He did not enjoy the work on the farm, and was always dreaming of all the other things he might be doing. He wanted to travel and see the world.

He knew that, when his father died, his money would be shared between his two sons. The younger son thought a lot about the good time he could have then. He could leave the farm to his brother and go right away from all the hard work.

The more he thought about it the more exciting it seemed. Now was the time to enjoy himself, while he was young. If only he could persuade his father to give him his share now. It was worth a try. He waited for a good opportunity before he talked to his father about it. Soon his chance came.

"It is much too dull working on the farm," he said. "I don't like the work and you don't really need me. You and my brother would get on just as well without me. Could I have the money you have put away for me so that I can go and see the world?"

His father was a kind man and he loved both his sons, but he looked at his younger son a little sadly. He was not sure whether it would be wise to give him his share soon. Yet he could see the lad would be unhappy if he were refused.

"Very well, son," he said. "If that is what you really want you can have the money. Be wise in the use you put it to."

A few days later the son set off with the money jingling in his bag. He had never felt so rich before. There was no end to the things he could do. He could live like a king for years.

He travelled a long way, seeing many wonderful things, making new friends and spending money freely. He bought new clothes and held gay parties and for a time he enjoyed himself enormously, doing many things he had never done before.

His money got less and less, but that did not bother him. He hardly noticed how quickly it was going. Life was good. Besides he was not spending all his money on himself. He had plenty of friends and he gave them money when they asked for it. They were always telling him what a jolly good fellow he was. He had almost forgotten what it

was like to work on a farm. In fact he had forgotten what it was like to work at all.

But the day came when there was no money left. Then all his friends drifted away. Gradually he had

to sell all that he had bought to pay for food. He had nothing to show for all the money with which he had started out. Now there were no gay times and no parties. He could no longer afford to buy clothes. None of his friends would help him, not even when he could not afford to buy food. He began to feel hungry. The time came when he knew that he would have to find some work or he would starve. But no one wanted him. There were not many things he could do, and the only job he could find was that of looking after pigs. The money he was paid for this was so little that he couldn't even buy himself enough food. Often he was so hungry he ate some of the pigs' food.

Now he found himself dreaming about how good life had been on his father's farm. He wished he had never left it.

"Even the servants have plenty to eat. They are never hungry and cold like I am," he said to himself.

The more he thought about his home, the more he longed to be there. One day he could bear it no longer, and he said to himself:

"I will go back to my father and will say to him: 'Father, I have sinned against God, and I have wasted your money. I do not deserve to be called your son. Please, may I work for you as a servant?'"

As soon as he could, he started the long journey home. After many days, when he was still quite a long way from the house, his father saw him coming over the hill, and ran to meet him. When they met, his father kissed him, and the son fell on his knees.

"Father," he said, "I have sinned against God and wasted all your money. I do not deserve to be called your son."

But his father did not let him say any more. He called his servants.

"Put out the best clothes for my son to wear. Put a ring on his finger and shoes on his feet. Let us have a feast and be glad because the son I had lost has come back to me."

When the other son came in from his work on the farm he was very angry and refused to go in. His father came out to him and begged him to come in. But his son said:

"All this time I have stayed and worked on the farm. I never did anything wrong. Yet you never made a feast like this for me."

"I know what you have done," said his father, "but my other son was lost and I thought dead. Can't you share my happiness that he is found and is alive?"

The Miraculous Catch of Fishes

ONE day Jesus borrowed his disciple Peter's boat. He taught the people from it, for there was a great crowd listening to Him from the shore.

When he had finished teaching, Jesus said:

"Launch out into the deep water and let down your net."

Peter told Jesus that they had fished all night and caught nothing.

"But," said Peter, "at your word, I will let down my net."

And when they had let down their net Peter and his brother

Andrew pulled it in again. It was so full of fish and so heavy that the net broke.

Then Peter and Andrew had to call to James and John and their friends to help them bring their great catch of fish to the shore.

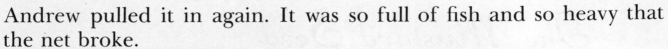

The Mustard Seed

NO one could tell stories better than Jesus and a crowd of people always gathered round him ready and eager to listen.

One day he told a story about a tiny little seed. Most seeds are so tiny that there are hundreds in one small packet. The seed which Jesus was talking about was the tiniest seed of all.

Often, as he went through the fields and farms with his disciples, he saw men and women sowing seeds in the good damp ground. Then the sun and the rain came to make them grow, and after a while little green shoots began to poke their heads through the ground. Day by day and month by month Jesus watched them grow until they became fine big plants.

The tiniest seed of all was called the mustard seed, and although this was so small, it grew and grew until it became a tree. Then the birds came and built their nests in its branches.

Jesus saw all this happening when he was out with his disciples. He remembered it when the people came crowding round him asking for a story.

On this particular day he told them about the mustard seed and how it grows into a tree.

"Such a tiny seed," he said, "it's so small it seems almost impossible that it could grow into a tree. Yet that is like God's kingdom. It starts like that tiny seed in your hearts when you begin to believe in Him, and as you learn more about Him and His great love, so that seed of belief grows and grows and you begin to tell others about Him and they also believe and then begin to tell others and so God's kingdom grows and grows."

Jairus's Daughter

ANOTHER day, while Jesus was preaching to a crowd of people, a man rushed through the crowd. Jesus saw him coming and knew that it was Jairus, one of the rulers of the Synagogue.

Jairus was breathless because he had been running, but as soon as he could speak he said to Jesus:

"Our little daughter is very ill. She is so ill that I am afraid she will die. Please come and lay your hands on her and then I know that she will live."

Jesus left the crowd of people who had been listening to him and went with Jairus. But many of the crowd followed them hoping to see another miracle.

Before they reached the house a messenger came running along the road to them.

"There is no need to trouble the Master any further," he said. "Your little girl is dead. Jesus can do nothing for her now."

Jesus, overhearing this, said to Jairus:

"Don't be afraid. Just believe in me."

Then he turned to the crowd and said:

"Don't follow us further, but go home."

He called Peter, James and John, and together they went on with Jairus. When they arrived at the house, there were many people crying and making a great noise. In those days it was the custom, when someone died, for people to come from all around to show how sorry they were.

When Jesus saw them he said:

"What is all this noise about? The little girl is not dead. She is just sleeping."

The crowd laughed at him because they were sure that she really was dead. Jesus sent them all out of the house and he took Jairus, and his wife, and the three disciples into the room where the little girl lay.

Jesus looked down at the little girl. Then, taking her by the hand, he said:

"Little girl, get up."

Straight away the little girl opened her eyes and got up.

Jesus turned to Jairus.

"Give your little girl something to eat, for she is hungry," he said.

Feeding the Five Thousand

AFTER these things had happened people began to follow Jesus everywhere.

One day, when he wanted to talk quietly to his disciples, he took them right away from the town to a place where they could be alone. But there were many people who wanted to hear what Jesus had to

say, and soon they found out where he had gone and followed him. Now, instead of there being just Jesus and the twelve disciples, there were Jesus, the twelve disciples, and a great crowd of people.

Time passed quickly as Jesus talked. Everybody was so interested that they stayed on and on, until at last they were very hungry.

The disciples came to Jesus to ask if they should send the people home.

"Give them something to eat first," said Jesus.

The disciples looked at Jesus in astonishment.

"We haven't the food or the money," they said. "It would cost a lot to feed all these people."

A boy who was standing near, heard the disciple talking about food. He thought of the basket beside him which his mother had packed before he left home. There was not much in it. Just five

barley cakes and two small fishes; only enough for him. But if Jesus needed them he would not keep them for himself.

He plucked up his courage and tugged at the sleeve of the disciple nearest to him. When the disciple looked down at him the boy was glad to see that it was Andrew, who was always friendly.

"What is it, son?" asked Andrew.

"I've got some cakes and fishes here," he said. "You could give those to Jesus and he could share them out among the people. It's not very much, but if Jesus had it there might be enough for some."

Andrew laughed as he looked into the basket.

"It won't go very far among this crowd," he said.

"Take it to Jesus and see," said the boy.

So Andrew took the basket to Jesus and said:

"There's a boy who says you can have his cakes and fishes."

"Thank you," said Jesus.

Then he turned to his disciples and said:
"Tell the people to sit down."
When Jesus had blessed the food he broke the cakes into pieces and divided the fishes. Then he called the disciples and told them to take the food round to the people. There was something for everyone, and they all ate until they were satisfied.
"Take these baskets and collect the pieces which are left," said Jesus to his disciples.
Each of the disciples took a basket and filled it with the pieces. When they returned to Jesus they were amazed to see that every basket was full.

Jesus Walks on the Water

ONE day Jesus told his disciples to go in the boat across the sea while he went up to the mountain to pray. It was evening before Jesus came down from the mountain. By that time the boat was in the midst of the sea, being tossed by waves, for the wind was very strong. The disciples were afraid. They crouched low in the boat, trying to shield themselves from the storm.

Suddenly one of the disciples pointed across the water. "Oh look," he cried. The others looked where he had pointed and could hardly believe what they saw. Someone was walking on the water. They were afraid. Then Jesus spoke to them: "Don't be afraid, it is I, Jesus."

"If it really is you, Master," said Peter, "let me come and walk on the water to you."

"Come, Peter," said Jesus. Peter climbed over the side of the boat and

started to walk on the water to Jesus. But when he felt the wind and waves beating against him he was afraid once more.

"Save me. Save me, Jesus," he called. "I'm sinking."

Jesus stretched out his hand and said:

"You haven't much faith, Peter. Don't you trust me?"

And he helped him back to the boat, and the wind ceased and the sea was calm once more.

Then all who were in the boat worshipped Jesus because they were sure, now, that he was the Son of God.

The Good Samaritan

A certain lawyer came to Jesus and asked Him,
"What must I do to go to heaven?"
Jesus answered:
"Love God with all your heart and mind, and love your neighbour as much as yourself."
The lawyer said:
"Who is my neighbour?"
Then Jesus told this story.

"A man was travelling to a town called Jericho. On the way robbers attacked him. They stole everything he had, took his clothes, wounded him badly and left him lying, half dead, by the road.

Later a priest passed by, but he left the poor traveller lying there and crossed to the other side of the road.

Then a Levite, a man who helped in the temple, came by. He too crossed over and did not help the poor wounded traveller.

The third man to pass was a Samaritan.

The Jews and the Samaritans were not friends and the people listening expected Jesus to say that the Samaritan would be hard-hearted too.

But Jesus continued:

"The Samaritan stopped. He picked up the poor man and tended his wounds with oil and wine to make the wounds heal. He put some of his own clothes on the traveller and took him on his donkey to an inn.

At the inn the Samaritan paid for the wounded man to be looked after. He promised he would come back and pay any more money that was owing."

Then Jesus asked the lawyer and the people listening:

"Which of all these men do you think was a neighbour to the man the robbers hurt?"
The lawyer replied:
"The Samaritan that helped him."
Jesus said:
"You must do the same for your neighbours."

The Lost Sheep

IN spite of all the things Jesus taught them, the Pharisees and leaders of the people either could not or would not understand how great is God's love. They still thought that Jesus ought not to have anything to do with the tax gatherers and others who did things which were wrong.

"Look at him," they said, when they saw him attracting such people. "He's letting all those wicked people follow him around. He ought to have nothing to do with them."

"He encourages them," said another man. "He even went to have supper with some of them the other night. That's a thing we would never do."

Jesus heard them grumbling among themselves about him.

"God's love reaches out to everyone," he said. "I'll tell you a story which will help you to understand this.

"There was once a shepherd who had a hundred sheep. Every day he took them out on the fields and hillsides and let them roam and look for fresh grass. Mostly they kept together as sheep do. Then one of them became a little venturesome. She wandered away from the rest of the flock looking for more tasty pieces of grass and scrub. Then, still further away, she saw some which looked even better. She wandered on and on

not noticing where she was going until she was so far away from the rest of the flock that she could not see or hear them.

"At the end of the day the shepherd came to take his sheep home. He counted them one by one as they went into the fold. There were only ninety-nine. One of them was missing.

"Now," said Jesus, "what would you have done if it had been your sheep that was missing? Would you have let her stay lost?"

The people who were listening knew they would not do any such thing. Each one of the sheep would be valuable to them, and they began to understand why Jesus was telling them this story. But they said nothing, so Jesus answered his own question.

"Of course you wouldn't," he said, "and neither did that shepherd. Although it was late he went straight off to find the missing sheep. He searched and searched, for she had wandered far during the day. At last he found her. Very gently he picked her up and laid her over his shoulder. He carried her all the way back to the fold.

"When he got back and had put her with the rest of the flock, he was so happy that he called all his friends together.

"'Come and rejoice with me,' he said, 'for I have found my sheep which was lost.'"

Then Jesus said to those who were listening:

"That is how it is with God. He loves everyone, no matter how bad they are. He is wanting them to give up their bad ways and become his friends and helpers."

The Widow's Mite

ONE day, when Jesus went into the temple, he stood near the offertory box. Rich people and poor came into the temple to worship and Jesus watched them putting their money into the box.

Then Jesus wanted to tell those people a story about giving. He called his disciples over to him. There were a lot of people around, so they heard the story too.

"When people come into God's temple," he said, "they give their money to help His work. Many people who come are rich. They have a lot of money so they can give a lot. Today I have seen some people put a lot of money into the box. They were the rich people.

"Then I saw a woman come in. She is a widow and lives alone and she has no one to work for her or help her. She was poorly dressed and I knew she had very little money, but she stopped at the offertory box and opened her purse. All she had was in that purse; just two small coins. They were not worth much, but she took them out and dropped them into the box."

The disciples were wondering why Jesus was telling them this. Then he surprised them by saying:

"Do you know, that woman really gave more than anyone else."

"How was that?" asked the disciples. "You said she only had two small coins to give."

"That is true, but those who were rich and gave a lot of money still had plenty left. It did not hurt them to give. They would hardly miss it. But this woman, this widow, who had so little, gave all she had."

Then the disciples remembered something that Jesus had said to a rich man a short time before. This man had come to him just as Jesus was going to start on a journey. He had kneeled at his feet asking Jesus to tell him what he ought to do to show that he loved God and his neighbour.

"Go and sell all that you have and give to the poor," Jesus had told him. "Then come and follow me."

The rich man was willing to do a lot of things, but he was not willing to give up his comforts and live a hard life following Jesus.

Then the disciples understood a little more what it meant to follow Jesus.

God
is
Love

Let us Pray

FOR what we are about to receive,
May the Lord make us truly thankful.
Amen

THANK you, Jesus, for the rain,
That beats upon the window pane.
It waters crops and makes them grow,
It makes the lovely flowers glow.
The thirsty birds can drink, and then—
Like me, praise God afresh, Amen

AWAY in a manger, no crib for a bed,
The little Lord Jesus laid down his sweet head.
The stars in the bright sky looked down where He lay,
The little Lord Jesus asleep in the hay.

The cattle are lowing, the Baby awakes,
But little Lord Jesus no crying He makes.
I love Thee, Lord Jesus! Look down from the sky,
And stay by my bedside till morning is nigh.

Be near me, Lord Jesus; I ask Thee to stay
Close by me for ever, and love me, I pray.
Bless all the dear children in Thy tender care,
And take us to Heaven to live with Thee there.

MARTIN LUTHER

TEACH me, my God and King,
    In all things Thee to see,
And what I do in anything,
To do it as for Thee.

GEORGE HERBERT (1593 – 1633)

WHAT can I give Him,
  Poor as I am?
If I were a shepherd
I would bring a lamb;
If I were a wise man
I would do my part,
Yet what can I give Him?
Give my heart.
  CHRISTINA GEORGINA ROSSETTI
          (1830 — 1894)

O PRAISE God in his holiness: praise Him in the firmament of his power.

Praise Him in His noble acts: praise Him according to His excellent greatness.

Praise Him in the sound of the trumpet: praise Him upon the lute and the harp.

Praise Him in the cymbals and dances: praise
   Him upon the strings and pipe.

Praise Him upon the well-tuned cymbals:
   praise Him upon the loud cymbals.

Let every thing that hath breath: praise
   the Lord.

PSALM 150

OUR Father, who art in Heaven,
    Hallowed be Thy name,
Thy Kingdom come,
Thy will be done in earth,
As it is in Heaven.
Give us this day our daily bread,
And forgive us our trespasses,
As we forgive them that trespass against us.
And lead us not into temptation;
But deliver us from evil:
For Thine is the Kingdom,
The Power and the Glory,
For ever and ever.
                    Amen.

DEAR Jesus, please bless all I do.
Help me do it well for you.
Bless the words I speak each day.
Make them cheerful, kind and gay.
Make me good in every way,
And if I *have* been naughty, then
Please help me to be good again!

ALL things bright and beautiful,
  All creatures great and small,
All things wise and wonderful,
The Lord God made them all.

Each little flower that opens,
Each little bird that sings,
He made their glowing colours,
He made their tiny wings.

The purple-headed mountain,
The river running by,
The sunset and the morning
That brightens up the sky.

The cold wind in the winter,
The pleasant summer sun,
The ripe fruits in the garden,
He made them every one;

The tall trees in the greenwood,
The meadows where we play,
The rushes by the water,
We gather every day;

He gave us eyes to see them,
And lips that we might tell
How great is God Almighty,
Who has made all things well.
CECIL FRANCES ALEXANDER (1818-1895)

JESUS, tender shepherd, hear me,
  Bless Thy little lamb tonight.
Through the darkness be Thou near me,
Keep me safe till morning light.

All this day Thy hand hast led me,
And I thank Thee for Thy care.
Thou hast clothed me, warmed me, fed me,
Listen to my evening prayer.

Let my sins be all forgiven,
Bless the friends I love so well.
Take me home at last to Heaven,
Happy there with Thee to dwell.

MARY L. DUNCAN

THE Lord is my shepherd, I shall not want.
   He maketh me to lie down in green pastures,
He leadeth me beside the still waters.
He restoreth my soul; He leadeth me in the paths of righteousness
For His name's sake.
Yea, though I walk through the valley of the shadow of death,
I will fear no evil:
For Thou art with me.
Thy rod and Thy staff, they comfort me.
Thou preparest a table before me in the presence of mine enemies.
Thou anointest my head with oil, my cup runneth over.
Surely goodness and mercy shall follow me all the days of my life,
And I will dwell in the House of the Lord for ever.

23rd PSALM

I SEE the moon, and the moon
sees me.
God bless the sailors on the sea.

THANK you for the world so sweet,
Thank you for the food we eat,
Thank you for the birds that sing,
Thank you, God, for everything.

E. R. LEATHAM

THE SELKIRK GRACE

SOME hae meat, and canna eat,
  And some wad eat that want it;
But we hae meat and we can eat,
  And sae the Lord be thankit.

ROBERT BURNS (1759-1796)

MATTHEW, Mark, Luke and
John,
      The Bed be blest that I
      lie on.
Four angels to my bed,
Four angels round my head,
One to watch, and one to pray,
And two to bear my soul away.

LAMB of God, I look to Thee,
Thou shalt my example be.
Thou art gentle, meek and mild,
Thou wast once a little child.

THE BLESSING

THE blessing of God Almighty,
the Father, the Son, and the
Holy Ghost,
Be amongst you and remain with
you always.
Amen.

LOVING Shepherd of Thy sheep,
Keep me, Lord, in safety keep.
Nothing can Thy power withstand,
None can pluck me from Thy hand.

DEAR God, bless all the animals;
    All creatures that you made,
Help *me* to help you care for them,
Don't let them be afraid,

Or hungry, or unhappy,
Or homeless; bless them all.
Help *me* to help whene'er I can,
Thy creatures great and small.

                              A.E.P.

OUR roses bloom and fade away,
   Our infant Lord abides alway.
May we be blessed his face to see,
And ever little children be.
                HANS CHRISTIAN ANDERSEN

HE prayeth best, who loveth best
All things both great and small;
For the dear God who loveth us,
He made and loveth all.

SAMUEL TAYLOR COLERIDGE (1772-1834)

DEAR God, be good to me;
The sea is so wide,
And my boat is so small.

(Breton fisherman's prayer)

BY God's fair air
I grind the grain;
Give ye good prayer
When bread ye gain.

LITTLE lamb, who made thee?
Dost thou know who made thee?
Gave thee life and bid thee feed,
By the stream and o'er the mead.
Gave thee clothing of delight,
Softest clothing, woolly bright.
Gave thee such a tender voice,
Making all the vales rejoice.

Little lamb, who made thee?
Dost thou know who made thee?

Little lamb, I'll tell thee.
Little lamb, I'll tell thee;
He is called by thy name
For He calls Himself a Lamb,
He is meek and he is mild,
He became a little Child.
I a child and thou a lamb,
We are called by His name.

Little Lamb, God bless thee.
Little Lamb, God bless thee.
(William Blake 1757-1827)

WHEN I'm fast asleep in my
little bed,
May sweet dreams fill my head.
The clock ticks on and very loud—
I'll dream of angels on a cloud.
Angels guard me whilst I sleep
And all my loved ones safely keep.
(J. Carruth)

O Jesus, I offer Thee this day
All my thoughts and work and play.
Let me be good as good can be,
Gentle, loving, kind like Thee.

TODAY, I have been simply horrid,
  Smashed some toys and torn a page—
Ripped my shirt and bumped my forehead,
Hit my brother in a rage.
Tomorrow, I'll do things for Mother,
Jesus, help me and I'll try;
Playing nicely with my brother,
Sorry that I made him cry.

A little old lady in a humble cot,
Said, "Jesus, thank You, for all I've got;
A tiny house and a garden plot,
To some folks it's little, to me it's a lot.

My pussy, my budgie, my mongrel Spot;
The daisies, the roses, the forget-me-not,
The rain, so fresh, the sun so hot.
Thank You, Jesus, for all I've got."

PRAISE God from Whom all blessings flow,
Praise Him, all creatures here below.
Praise Him above, the heavenly host,
Praise Father, Son and Holy Ghost

(St. John)

ALL good gifts around us
Are sent from Heaven above,
So thank the Lord, O thank the Lord,
For all His love.

(J. Montgomery Campbell)

A Child's Grace

HERE a little child I stand,
Heaving up my little hand.
Cold as paddocks though they be
Here I lift them up to Thee
For a benison to fall
On our meat and on us all.

(Robert Herrick 1591-1674)

LOVING Jesus, gentle lamb,
In Thy gracious hands I am,
Make me, Saviour, what Thou art.
Live Thyself within my heart.
(Charles Wesley)

LORD, protect me through the night,
And bring me safe to morning light;
If I should die before I wake,
I pray the Lord my soul to take.

A Cowboy's Prayer

LORD, shield me from the blazing sun,
  And let me find a water hole;
Protect me from the rustler's gun,
And dust storms in the desert bowl.
And when I reach the prairies' end,
Where dues are paid and comrades part,
Let me remember the Lord's my Friend
And thank Him with a grateful heart.

BE present at our table, Lord.
Be here and everywhere adored.
Thy creatures bless, and grant that we
May feast in Paradise with Thee.

(John Wesley)

O Jesus, I have promised to serve Thee to the end;
Be Thou for ever near me, my Master and my Friend.
I shall not fear the darkness, when Thou art by my side.
Be Thou for ever near me, my Guardian and my Guide.